The Rizzler
Written by Tommy Watkins

I'm the kind of guy that wants to settle down.

Everywhere I turn, I see beautiful women. I want to talk to them but don't know how.

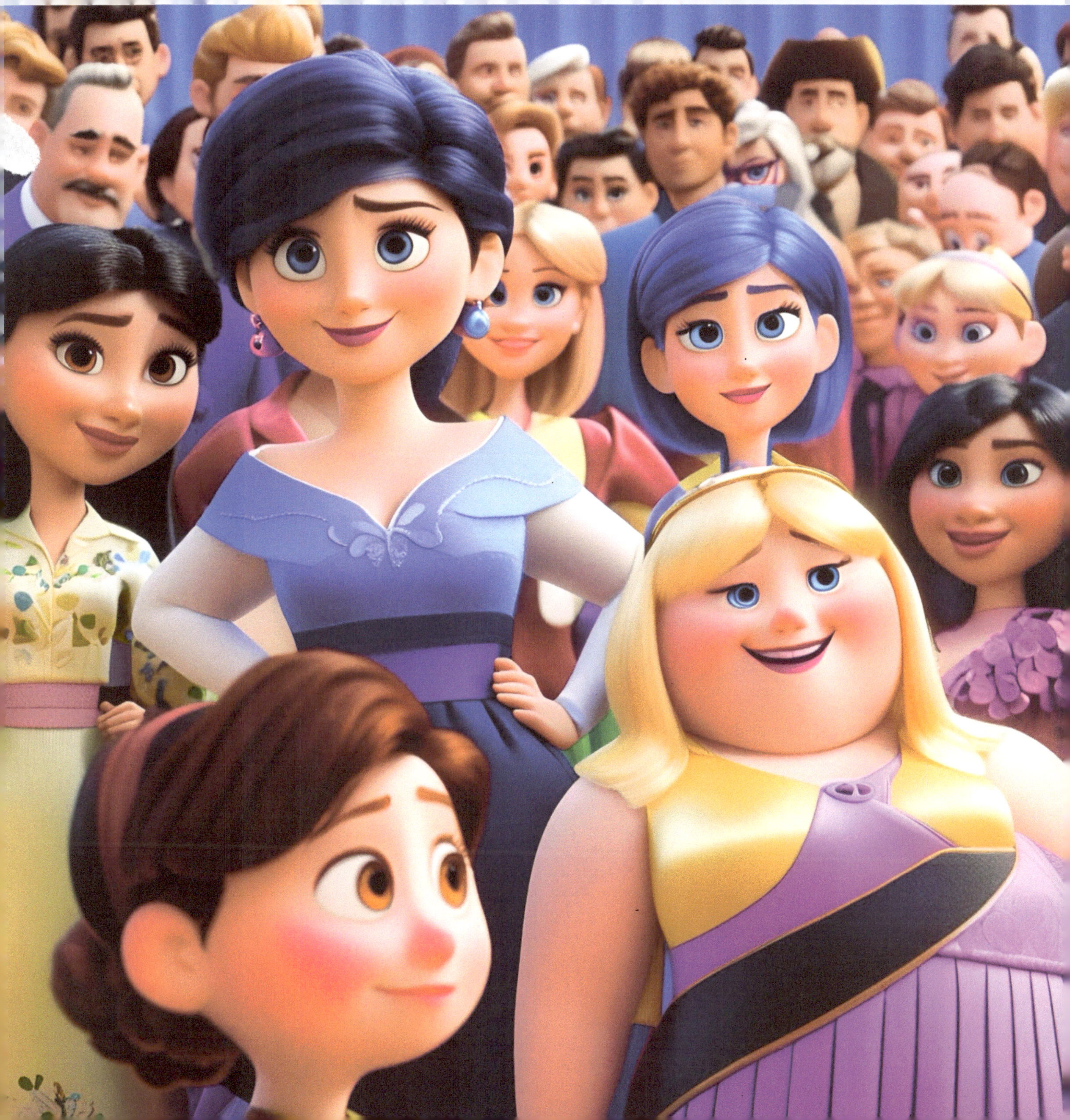

My friend told me I got to have Rizz.

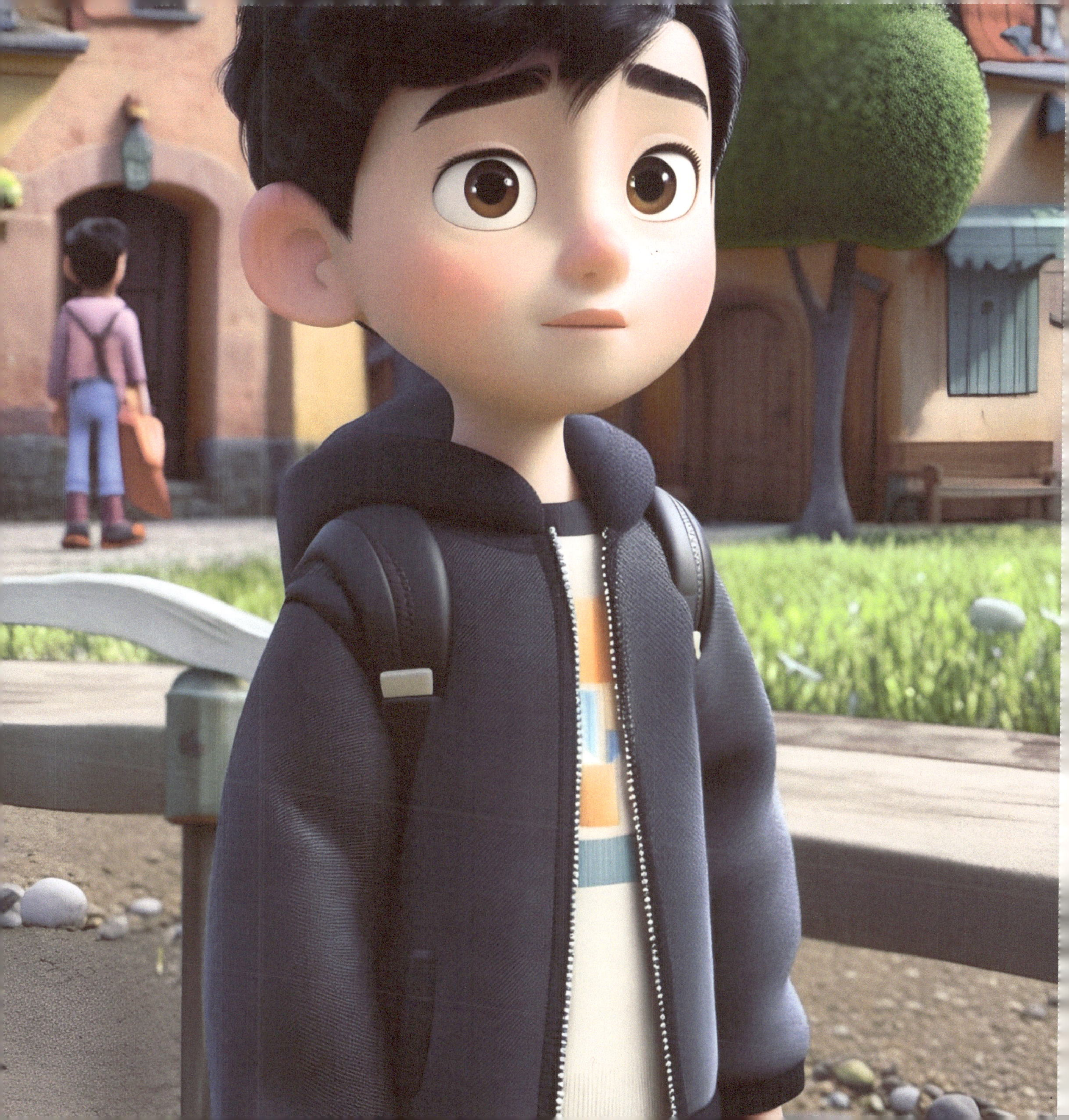

I don't know the first thing about Rizz or what it is. To show off to my friends, I walk up to a pretty girl with my phone camera on.

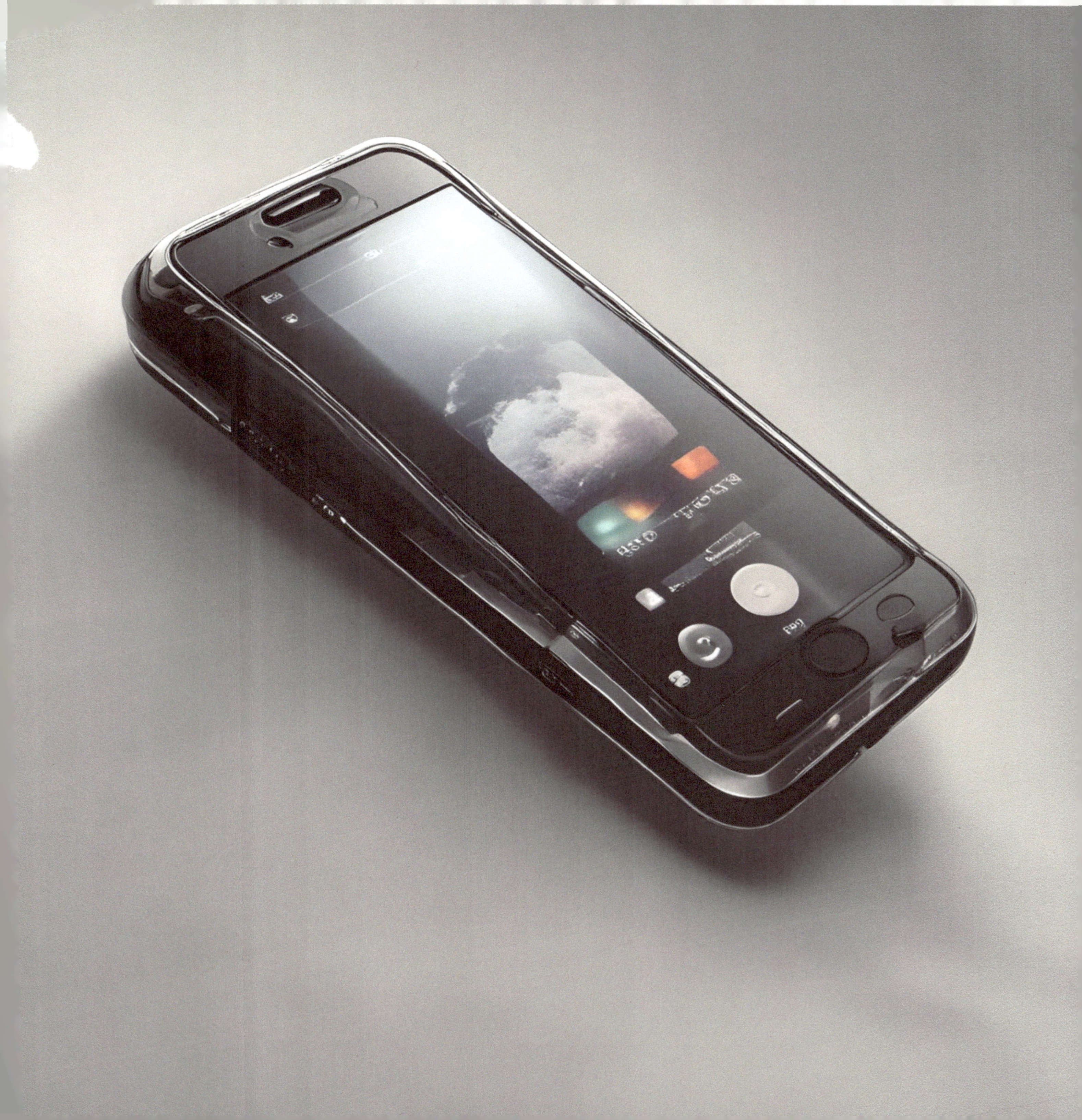

If I can record my interaction with her and she blows me off, at least I will go viral on social media.

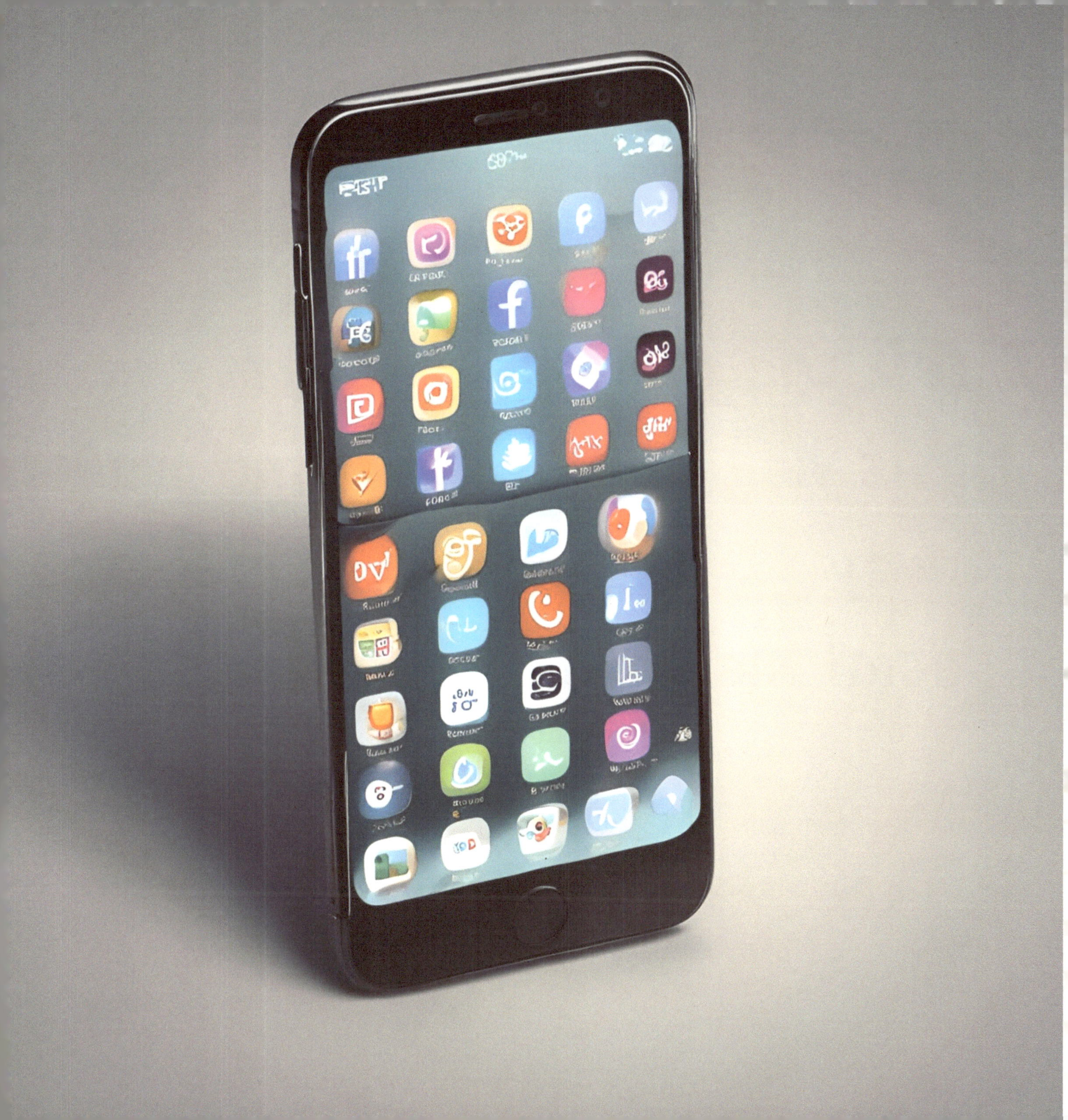

I tell the girl she is pretty. She turns her back to me and walks away. I posted that video to social media and only received five views.

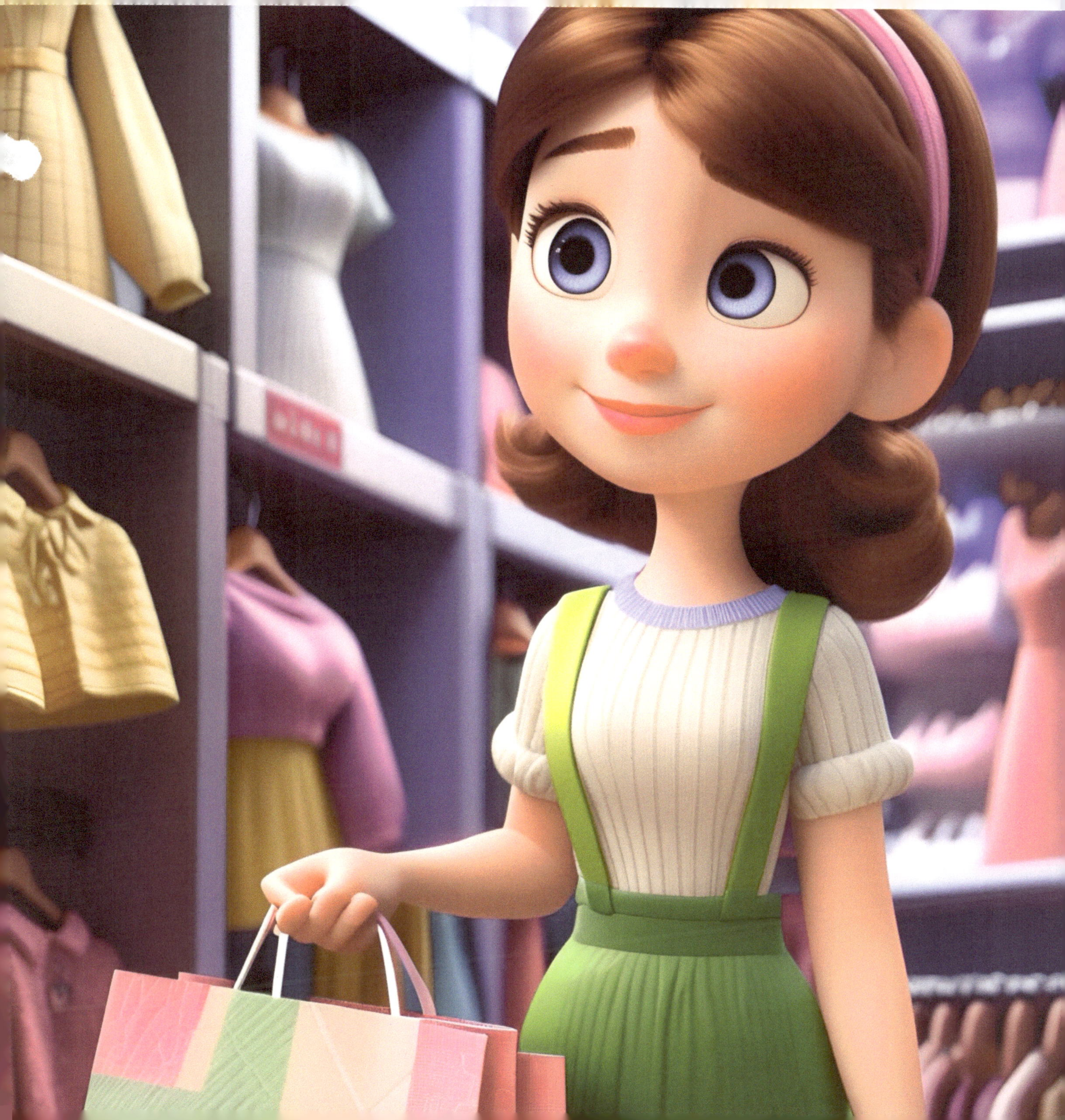

Fine, whatever, I will try my luck with the local bartenders. Bring my Rizz to the local bar.

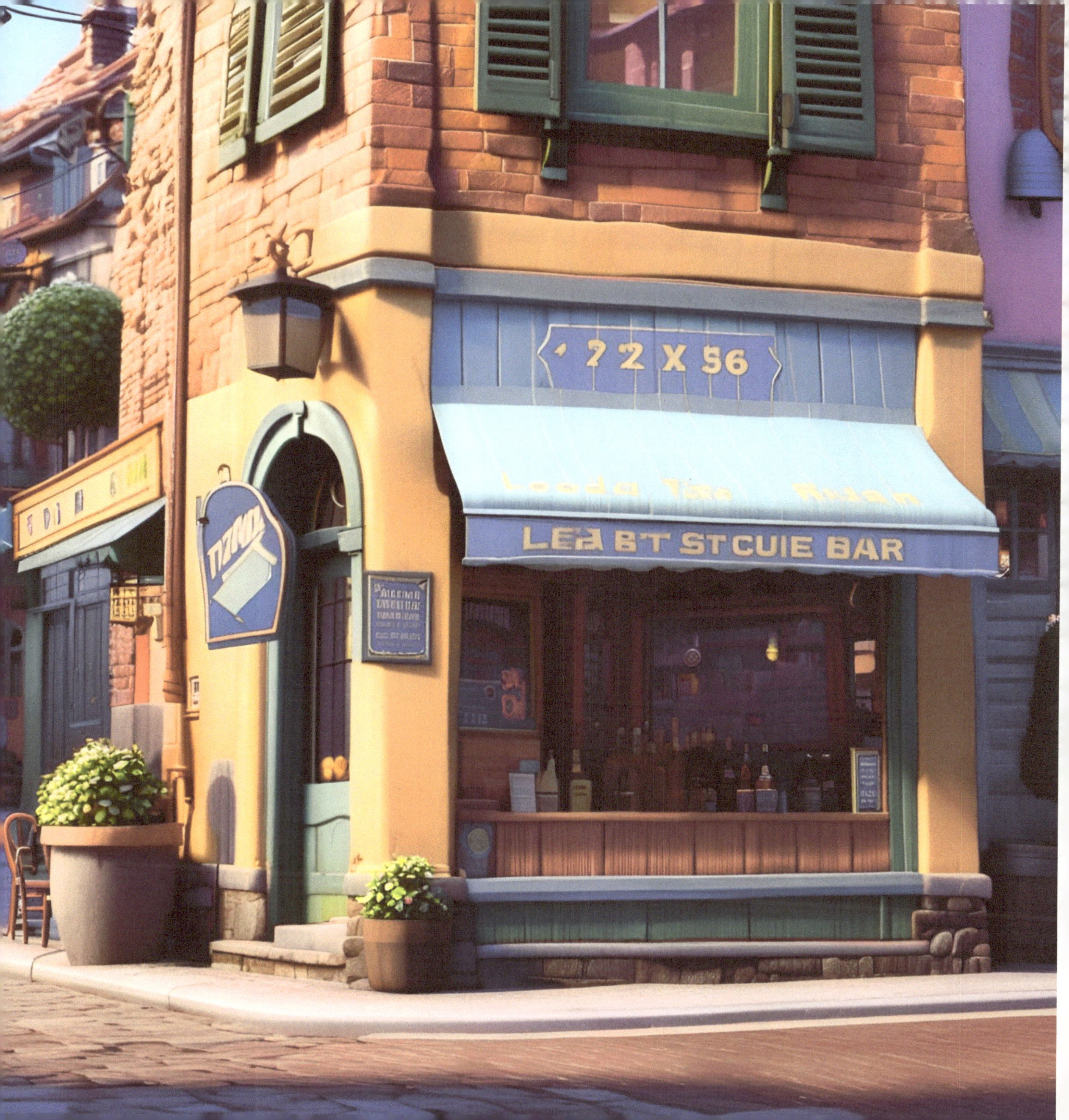
72 X 56

I go to the local bar, drink too much, and stumble home.

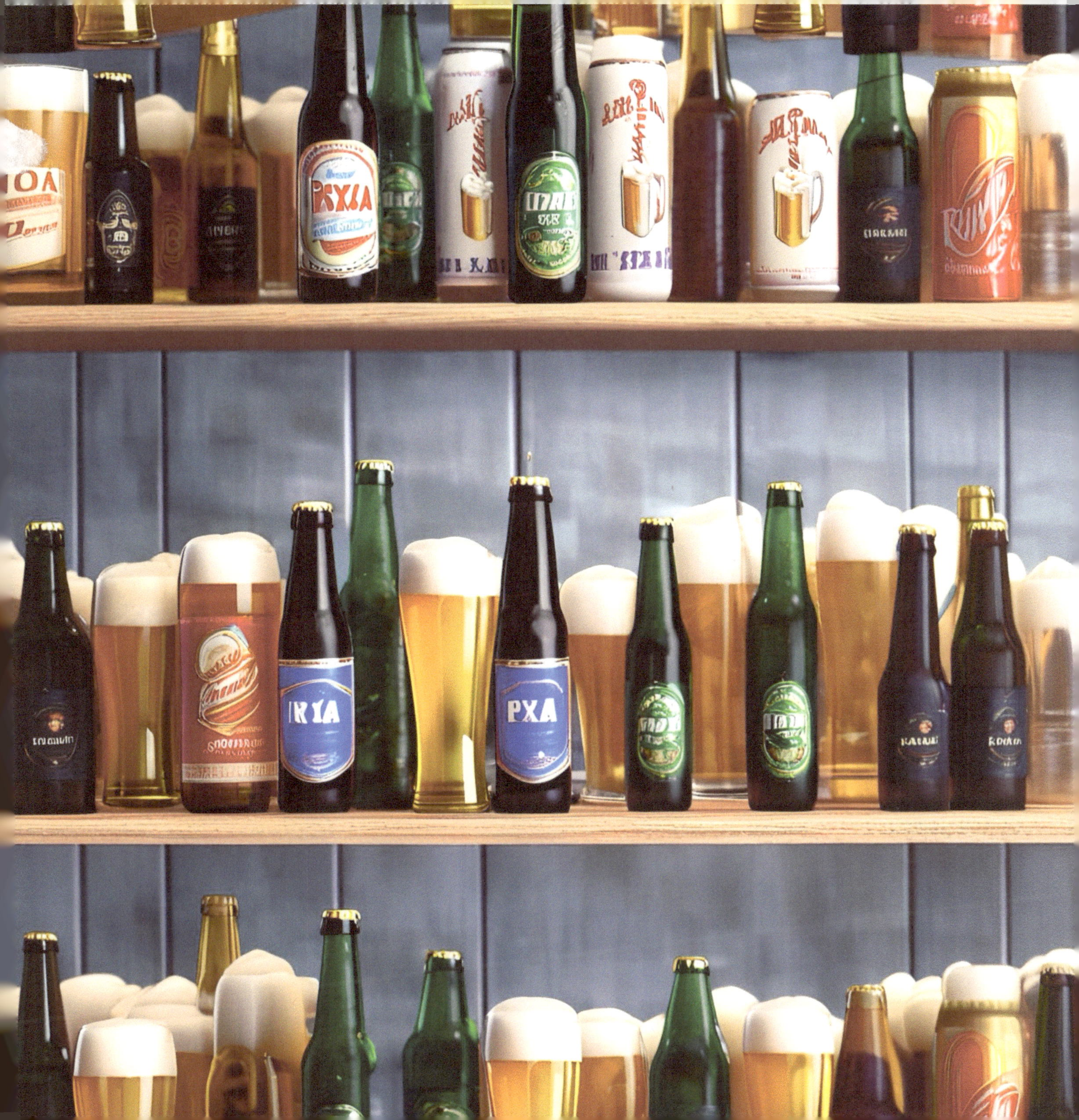
PXA

The next day, I head to my local coffee shop.

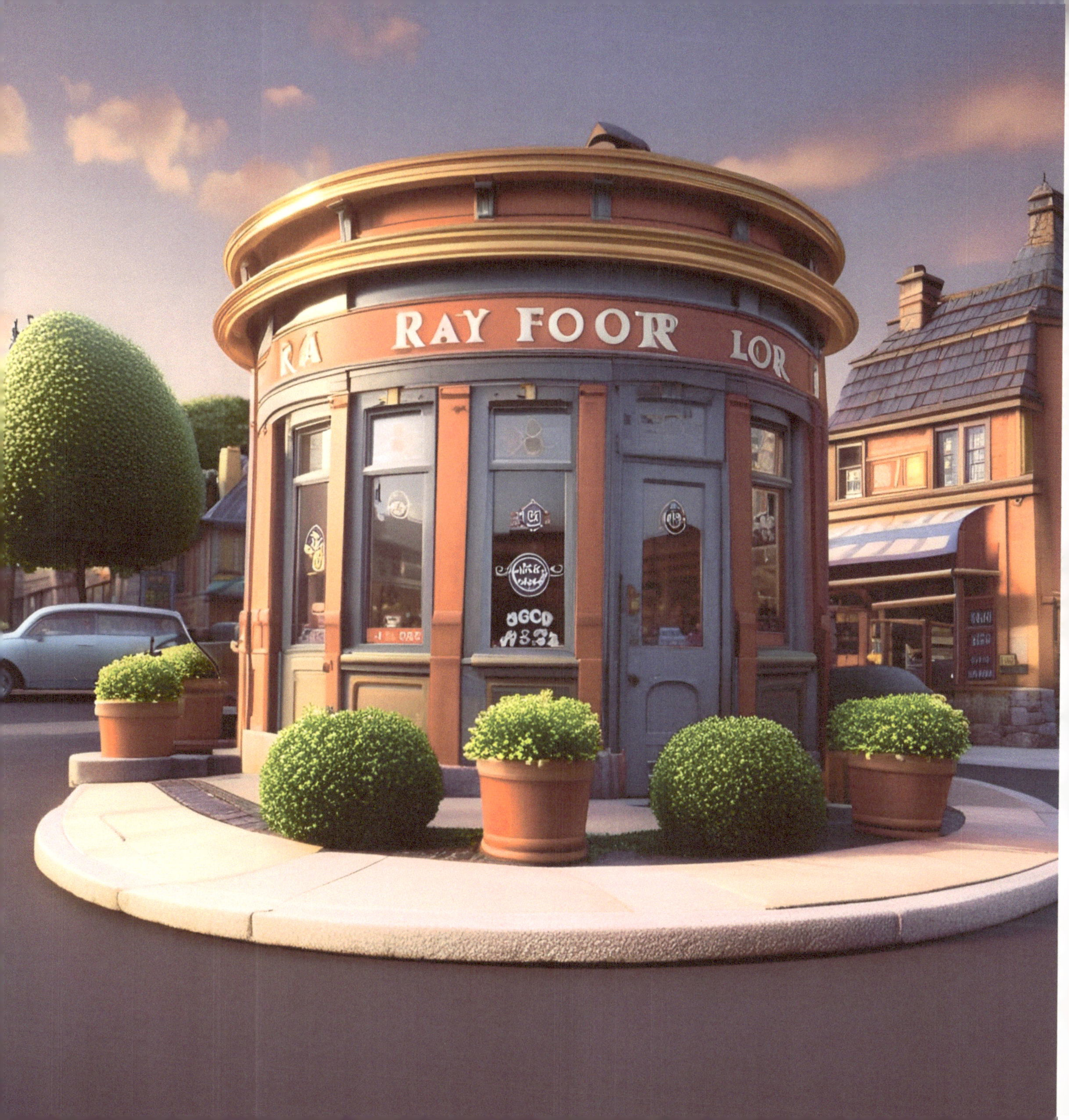
RA
RAY FOOR
LOR

There she is, sitting there drinking a coffee. Here's my chance to go for it. Forget the Rizz. I'm just going to be myself

The End

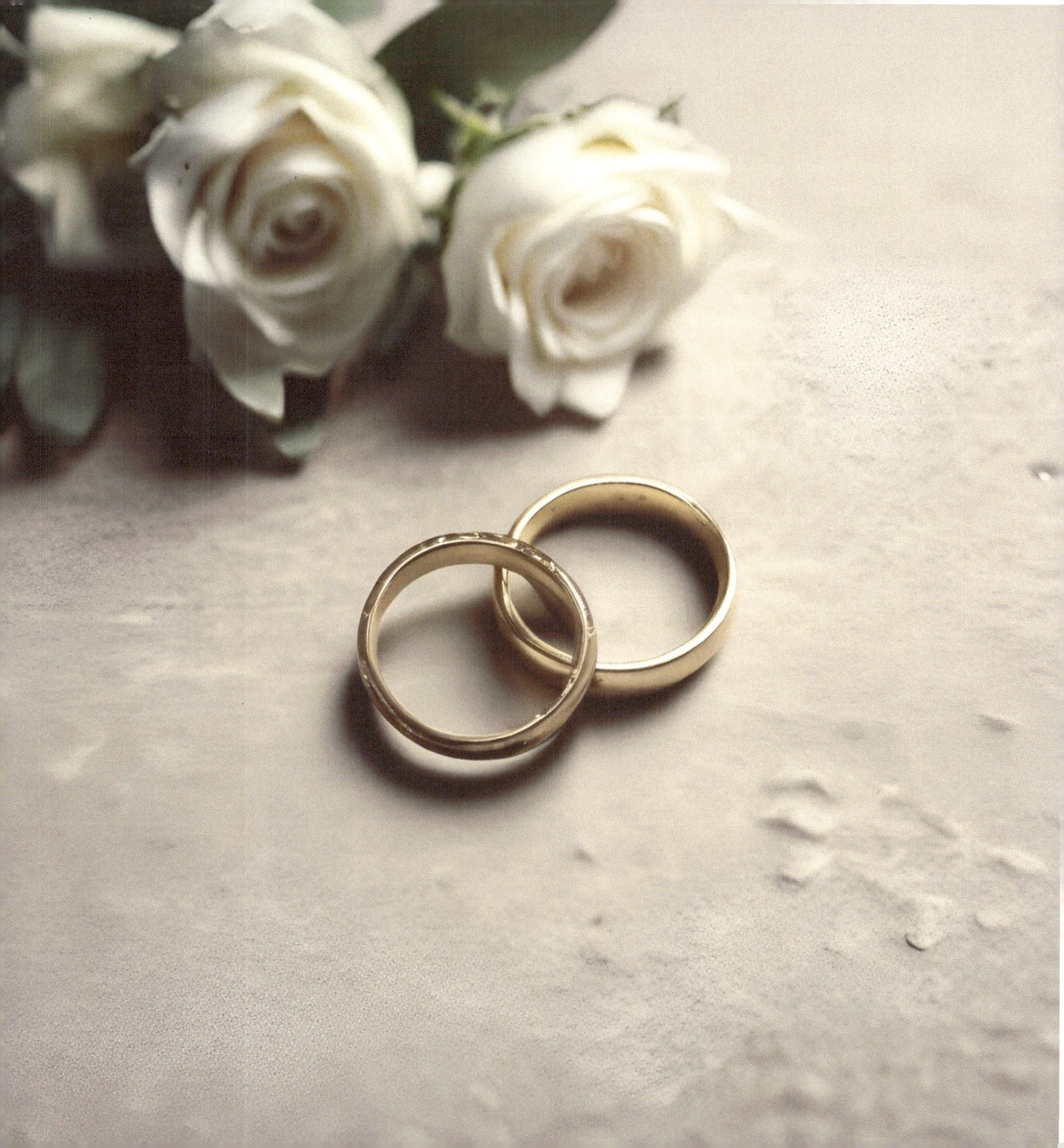

Milton Keynes UK
Ingram Content Group UK Ltd.
UKHW051307050724
445024UK00009BA/13